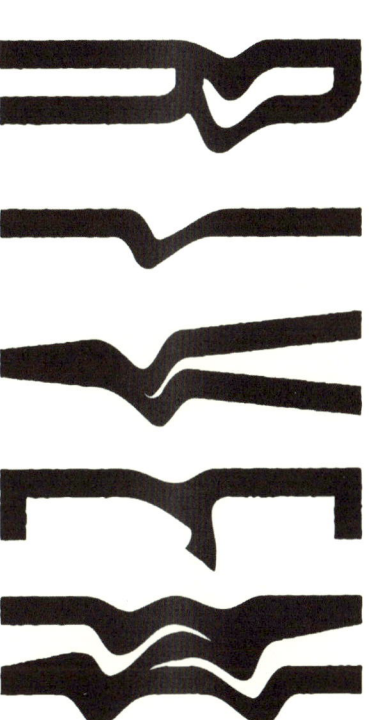

POEMS

CATHERINE OWEN

a misFit book

Copyright © Catherine Owen, 2020

Published by ECW Press
665 Gerrard Street East
Toronto, Ontario, Canada M4M 1Y2
416-694-3348 / info@ecwpress.com

All rights reserved. No part of this publication may be reproduced, stored in a retrieval system, or transmitted in any form by any process — electronic, mechanical, photocopying, recording, or otherwise — without the prior written permission of the copyright owners and ECW Press. The scanning, uploading, and distribution of this book via the Internet or via any other means without the permission of the publisher is illegal and punishable by law. Please purchase only authorized electronic editions, and do not participate in or encourage electronic piracy of copyrighted materials. Your support of the author's rights is appreciated.

Editor for the Press: Michael Holmes/ a misFit book
Cover design: Brienne Lim
Author photo: © Michael Belandiuk

LIBRARY AND ARCHIVES CANADA CATALOGUING IN PUBLICATION

Title: Riven : poems / Catherine Owen.

Names: Owen, Catherine, 1971- author.

Description: "A misFit book."

Identifiers: Canadiana (print) 20190236647
Canadiana (ebook) 20190236655

ISBN 978-1-77041-524-9 (softcover)
ISBN 978-1-77305-513-8 (PDF)
ISBN 978-1-77305-512-1 (EPUB)

Classification: LCC PS8579.W43 R58 2020
DDC C811/.54—dc23

The publication of *Riven* has been generously supported by the Canada Council for the Arts which last year invested $153 million to bring the arts to Canadians throughout the country and is funded in part by the Government of Canada. *Nous remercions le Conseil des arts du Canada de son soutien. L'an dernier, le Conseil a investi 153 millions de dollars pour mettre de l'art dans la vie des Canadiennes et des Canadiens de tout le pays. Ce livre est financé en partie par le gouvernement du Canada.* We acknowledge the support of the Ontario Arts Council (OAC), an agency of the Government of Ontario, which last year funded 1,737 individual artists and 1,095 organizations in 223 communities across Ontario for a total of $52.1 million. We also acknowledge the contribution of the Government of Ontario through the Ontario Book Publishing Tax Credit, and through Ontario Creates for the marketing of this book.

PRINTED AND BOUND IN CANADA   PRINTING: COACH HOUSE   5   4   3   2   1

"Consider rivers/they are always en route to their own nothingness/from the first moment/they are going home"
— EAVAN BOLAND

"I've come home, river: nothingness/returns to nothing"
— FAN WU

For Chris Matzigkeit [1981–2010]
though lost, always present.

Contents

Thirty-Six Sentences on the Fraser River that Could Serve as a Very Small Nest 11

Nature Writing 101 13

Beseech 14

To the Artist of Twenty-First Century Canadian Nature Painting 15

Fraser River, Thanksgiving 2011 16

"Who can say why or how it all blazed away" 17

Two Stanzas in Autumn 18

Meditation by Water 19

Earth Day 2012 20

Dusk from the Fourteenth Floor: a Pastoral Elegy 21

Let us look at the silver river 25

I have not brought you to this river for nothing 26

Though the duck, passing through the glittering span 27

As the crow drops down from the roof and over 28

I miss you says the river, and this is a difficult proposition 29

Every day I go to find you & every 30

Ice first and then mist and the river passes 31

The morning after it wasn't morning anymore 32

Sundays, in the frozen construction site 33

Suddenly, it's mid-December — the river 34

The inexorable, the river, and the sounds 35

And now a swan by the shipyards, an otter 36

They will disappear these ruins and this beauty too 37

Today the river is thick with wind 38

A tug passes and the river frays, splits 39

Lots of trains today, their whistles 40

Given respite this morning 41

Difficult today, the tears — and I see the river 42

You make me ache river with your — let me say it 43

Crow cries fall like snow after the snow 44

Come to the window — you call to me 45

The beach all geese today, slow sun dropping by 46

Sweetheart, I say to the river — good morning beautiful 48

They call it a brownfield, but of course today 49

Always, on opening your eyes, you gasp — 50

A strange amber stain on the river this morning — what is it — 51

Does the river need me, I wonder 52

Happy Valentine's Day river and you too of course 53

The river is so beautiful today I have no choice 54

A short line of ducks flying fast 55

Achingly beautiful — I understand this now — 56

The rain, machines but I remember — 57

And what if, after all this, river 58

The Last Aubade 59

Conniption: The River 63

One Haiku; Four Takes 65

One January Morning 66

Catch & Release 67

Reversals 68

One History of the Fraser 69

"Love should not be written in stone, but in water" 71

What they call this 72

Phantomnul 73

The River System 74

Acknowledgements 83

Thirty-Six Sentences on the Fraser River that Could Serve as a Very Small Nest

           after Crispin Elsted

1. Living by the river is not close enough.
2. Crows cross the river; swallows sip; geese nestle in.
3. If I could only hear the river flowing from where I am.
4. The river is like your death; it just keeps moving away from me.
5. *Everyone recognized him/except the river*, wrote Charles Lillard, but somehow I feel known here.
6. At dawn, the river's currents are dark as ice floes and they never cease.
7. River is to rivet as mesmerize is to memory.
8. I want to say *river river river river river* as King Lear did.
9. Where the sun swells in the river, silver as if you could bathe in it.
10. It is the longest river in this land: breadths & depths beyond the tributaries.
11. The heron, lifting off from a pylon, cries like the river would.
12. Rivers, you know this, have no particular desire to see you fail, but nor are they, otherwise, invested.
13. Li Po had something to say about rivers.
14. The discovery of the Fraser River in 1808 began with disappointment; it appeared to be unnamed.
15. You would still be alive if you could have lived above this river.
16. Salmon and sturgeon flip the thick coins of their bodies in the river; hooks from the banks curve into them.
17. The river smells of nothing sometimes: at others, creosote, or salt, faint.
18. Through a spider's web, the river seems to shudder.
19. Hurt, by the river, hurt.
20. When the tide pulls back, the river is almost all ruins.

21. The river holds the trees in two ways: as long dark hives, as booms.
22. From the mill: concrete, rebar, a discarded crane; from walkers: butt ends, Styrofoam, plastic remnants and one ditched bouquet.
23. No, not the river.
24. The distance between the North Sask River and the Fraser is how far you will have to travel from your death to where I am now living.
25. Through a ladybug I cannot see the river.
26. Fitting countries into the river, calculating hectares, metres, species, rates of flow: still.
27. As the sun advances, a million insects of light float down the river.
28. O river, o, o.
29. Tugs & fishing boats live in another century on the river, birds in the forever of it.
30. To see what I mean, you just have to spend hours with your eyes on the river, whether or not you witness.
31. Gold gathered us around this river and now too, gold.
32. The river, it begins me.
33. There was Lethe; there was Styx; where is the river of remembering?
34. *Heavily exploited by human activities,* says Wikipedia. The river glistens.
35. Alongside the river, machines tunnel through the mud: erect houses; everything we are releases toxins: the development is called New Water.
36. At the end of the epic, she said *yes*; I am saying *river.*

Nature Writing 101

Our minds can turn anything romantic.
Is the problem.
The sewagy mud of the Fraser a quaint muslin and the spumes

        pulsing out of chimneys at the Lafarge cement plant look,
        at night, like two of Isadora Duncan's scarves, pale, insouciant veils,
        harmless. The trees are all gone but then aren't our hearts

more similar to wastelands.
We can make it kin, this pollution, children we are sad about, their
delinquency linked to our own, irreparable with familiarity, a lineage of stench and

        forgiveness. Our minds can assimilate all horrors.
        Is the problem.
        The animals will disappear and those small, strange invertebrates;

the bees will vanish and in the well-oiled waters, fish
will surge their deaths over the sand bags.
But then we keep saying, "Let's construct another narrative."

        The nightmares must simply be called reality.
        And after this you see
        it is possible to carry on.

Beseech

Prolong me along the estuary
    where the cataclysmic wildflowers, all their poppy-joy-vermillion
smitten in pointillist manifold burgeon
    and there are discarded rust hungers too beautiful not to be
unwedged from granite and shouldered home, such bolts & rivets of ruin
    have we here below the swallow, tidbit draughts of slight salt water
and slim oil from the tug-lovely voyages, green peeling barges, power boats
    and the occasional Sea-Doo though the fishing lines continue to fall
from the small dreams of wharves while toddlers bucket & cry on shorelines
    passed by the endless joggers. O prolong me along the estuary there
is something in this thin stretch of eelgrass & bulrushes where the tide
    skew-wiffs in against the slow-eroding boardwalk
that is hope-solemn, proven re-tuning of what has been somewhat death-struck-
    numb and now wants, if living is what it does
to be vole-slickery and gold-holy as those dandelions tall beside the Fraser
    and of their origins, stone, perhaps, or song.

To the Artist of Twenty-First Century Canadian Nature Painting

No, you can't stop me from believing in beauty.
My only grief that I cannot give you the vision entire —

even if I were the sweet brooding painter of the Algonquin
I wouldn't be able to gift you with this river, its silver twists,

the slow shallows of minnows & light, the way tugs in dark knots
shepherd booms to the bridge past mangled rebar dancing

in its moored concrete chunks, the sandbar littered with swallow
prints and the eagle who slips back to its nest with the dripping

wiggle of a vole in its talons, just above the grey-roofed shipyard,
banked by green & gold barges and men who know how to leap.

No, even if I were shy, wild Tom Thomson with his colour-hyphenated
boards and cast-iron eggs camping by Canoe Lake that last summer

in wartime, I wouldn't be able to capture the particular, ragged
wonder of this beautiful, polluted river moving in all its histories

past us, the crumbling sawmill haunting with creosote and the persistent
singing of crickets and the Starbucks detritus and the watery receptions of stars.

Fraser River, Thanksgiving 2011

Thick winch of ripped rope at the base of a rusted bolt;
                beside it, a skimpy alder sapling,
all sprouting from a relic of fallen log, saw marks chunked with dirt

& clover. These the juxtapositions I live for — even the meagre beach
                is rich if you like ruins, not of the Thermopylae variety
but simpler dregs, a wrecked mill casting its rivets & cement

upon the scuzzy shoreline, even a deceased lobster resembling less
                a fleshly crustacean and more something hewn by giant,
discarded machines now lying in barbaric remnants on the edge of cornflowers

& cricket-song. A scow passes the dereliction, a tug and then waves ruck
                over estuary mud, prod sandpipers back on the half
mouldering wharf, roll geese in and in.

"Who can say why or how it all blazed away"
Anne Compton

The river has no silence in it or else it has silence but small.
You see the geese in a slow trail and think it will be forever

— why did he use the word forever. You get a moment, that is all,
steeping in the minor peace of their passing, golden, crying out

at intervals — this too being silence — before noise inserts itself:
the intercoms of tugs communicating their booms, a speedboat churning

the waters with its wahoo cargo, dogs busting onto the beach, ripping
through the tideline and the geese lift, rag themselves into a panic,

skitting to shipyard and pylons. Why did you imagine there could be
solace lasting at least longer than this — so much industry here and the historical,

how could this river ever know silence, a minute, that is it, of geese
moving with the current in their interpretable consolation and he not gone.

Two Stanzas in Autumn

Yellow orange blue grey over the waters
The trees in the never of themselves
What do I have to say to you anymore everything
Heave of giant missing a perfume a toxin
Beautiful absentee man; beautiful absentee river
I sing to you this is all I have.

*

Silver of the waters: machined silver; silvery road after rain
The trees become their antipathies, their secret selves
What can be a summation of your existence nothing
Swell of vast longing a poison an elixir
Sweet disappeared man; sweet disappearing river
I sing to you this is all I have.

Meditation by Water

When I think of you I think of the river —
the raw moment we had together
and that all before the driftwood skiff

of your body moved down the estuary, disappeared.
Now mountains crag out of the cloud line, a tug creates
an ocean as, in passing, it foists waves upon the small &

shrinking beach. Then there is a heron, or none, and a silence
that has crows, the shipyard and a dog in it. I am usually
alone here, neither empty nor full most days but waiting

for what cannot be waited for and so is beautiful futility
though you do return to me in a way as when I think of the river
I am not wholly never not thinking of you.

Earth Day 2012

There is everything now, at nearly the end of April, or almost everything
        out of the all   we have left: crows &

        geese, ladybugs & spiders, Indian plum

& cherry blossom and now the swallows
        return, a tan-blue zag of them over
                the river, speeding up the air towards
                summer, their wings,

as they cursive around me, are pleating with light — their beaks slide into
    drainpipes,
        their bodies slip within stucco holes where the small cargo of nests

                      waits.

As if I had not imagined anything like this
        before — the Earth given back to itself each year, generous

    despite our lessenings

            and the machines almost prostrate themselves before
            this power

that has nothing to do with forgiveness, that hushes grief.

Dusk from the Fourteenth Floor: a Pastoral Elegy

1.

Cigarette smoke, dinner whiffs, a Sikh security guard passing
  the perimeters of the insulated,
wooden chambers recently sold for untidy sums.

2.

Fathers roped into the evening push their kids on revolving
  pink machines, a clutch of joggers
tighten the path between railyard & road, crows, gauging them.

3.

Couples, gut-busted at the burger joint, waver out to their conveyances,
  cottonwoods silver,
dead blackberries roll up their pissed-on fruit.

4.

Volleyballers in fluorescent uniforms bat a pale punctuation mark
  over the nets at the faux-beach,
a few gulls doodle past, thistle flowers fluff.

5.

Log booms take the sun on their backs, water glams, early
  autumn of the neglected trees, tugs
making the river slash itself up & around the pier.

AUBADES

VANCOUVER, BC

Let us look at the silver river

Let us look at the silver river — it is not a dwelling here, it is a moving through —
    it has no alibis; its design is pure.
Do you know anymore what this means?

You can't accept it sometimes — there is the mother & the father — they
    were eternal with patience, a soft enduring glow — or else they are
ashes, only and silence — either way,

    the river trembles beneath the bridge and down to the mouth and then —

it becomes salt. You cannot stop it. Saltless & tar, it becomes salt & oil and both
    its bodies hold jetsam, the death of one cold child
caught in the current, un-basketed, and the tugboat drivers who find it, their

hands — their hands pouring into the silver river, drawing a body from a
    body and all the anonymous stars above. Let us look at the silver river because
this is nothing if not the end of us, he

not knowing who I was, ever, though traces of grocery lists, poorly
    scrawled letters, a slow look before sleep said much — what can it say
really, the trees, winter-sparse on the banks and then a heron or other bird

whose grey calm grows further & further away
    from what is built and maintained — such strange adherents of
sticking to place, ravaging it — as if we could stay here forever

                                                   watching.

I have not brought you to this river for nothing

I have not brought you to this river for nothing and not for death though some days
        you want stones to fill all the hollows in your past and in that way
vanish —
        a black swash of crows taking off from the muddy field, leaving for one
ghost forest or another and the pulled velour wake the water makes when
                                      confronted —

I can't tell you how to heal me or if this is possible — they will remove

        all these ruins, you say, it is a liability after all — though better the rebar
                & kindling,
a solo stray pumpkin lolling back and forth on the isthmus amid old nets,
        copper wire,
        than the puerile hope that no one will suffer

and beginning — beginning again following all this tidal discussion — what can
        I tell you —
        the hulls are bleached in the shipyard and I feel sorrow

about not being able to and the light, how it touches here & there until
                noon on us, then
        moves behind that memory of him

                        when a small boy, blond he was as sand

and the eroded day, the narrative of then and then and then, it was there you see,
        already.

Though the duck, passing through the glittering span

Though the duck, passing through the glittering span of water appears
to vanish, it does not and on the other side emerges, two delicate

traces of movement trailing from its pinions — others land later and the fire
consumes them too — the next day though is cold and fog hunkers down over

the pylons — the river resists me like trying to remember him
alive sometimes — there is his hand grabbing for the coffee mug but not

>   legs holding him up while he does this
>   — where are his legs?

His smile lives in me certain days, a few indeterminate gestures, but his voice,
his voice has drowned — O look, someone has left a lipstick by the path,

there a fragment of clothing, unreadable, all balled up like that, random — I
acknowledge transience and then this passes too

>   and the rage, rage, rage is back, just
>   squatting

on a plank by the waterline's discrepancies.
No, I haven't forgotten you.

>   Yes, you're going to have to wait.
>   Again.

As the crow drops down from the roof and over

As the crow drops
                down from the roof and over the closed river — sealed today
with December, a slow imagination of ice
                      — you are too sweet with me and ingratiating —
there is no getting beyond how we commingled in what we thought was simplicity
      but that now we see is — all the winches, the crazy saws, the fact you
cannot report to the site without a hard hat, steel toed boots
                      and an ignorance of the names of birds

      — one is otherwise, too distracted — and now I wonder what fish they
                catch from all the thin piers in summertime
and how they reel them in so easily, strip them, eat them in pieces like
      that — I have tried to say many times — this is about the river
           and yes, the poem — when the geese flew past us that
                afternoon you turned,
briefly,
      scanned the documents of their wings, while he would complain always
           about the cold

so neither of you know how my heart is ripped through by that vee, utterly and
            changed
                not cleanly, did I pretend this.

No.

I miss you says the river, and this is a difficult proposition

I miss you says the river, and this is a difficult proposition — haven't I sat acolyte
    at his shores so often they have come
calling for me — there are obviously other meanings to this washing in
    & out of the heavily wooden waters, the cries of birds that flap

        canvas wings, landing with wire legs
in the deep & dirty sand — don't tell me

this is happening again —
        the harems in the mind and the hurt boys on the shore — I
        can't handle a domestic
empire — did I ever mention an Easy-Bake Oven was included
        in my last testament? —

the silver river curves around its log booms, curves around its boats
        and cranes and piers —
    the movement here is inclusive or, perhaps, indifferent —
sometimes, I can be like that, or want to, or repeat this is who I am
    while all the time if there

could be a nest reserved for me in the highest pine above the estuary, I'd be in it
    so fast,
        singing little ditties, waiting for you

                to return.

Every day I go to find you & every

Every day I go to find you and every time bring something back —
                once it was crows, or the light only on that part of the river and

wishing this could all stay wasteland you see, which is less than Eden but more than
                people — the only real cultivators of darkness,

fumes and ditching things on the side of the road,
                a nostalgia that makes even addiction quaint

on occasion — so just give me a rough little cove with driftwood
                & sunsets, some of those piquant white flowers that tear through

stone so growing old won't be that difficult —
                without you, I mean —

though, at the same time, the starlings in the muddy field alight and there is the
    impartial in this; they pick among the river's winters

                                          ; they move on.

Ice first and then mist and the river passes

Ice first and then mist and the river passes from harsh demarcations
        to none — like that — in the span of an hour or two I think —

I wake up frequently to wonder why he's not there — my body does, my brain
        knows better — or is it the other way around — walking the sloppy trail

to the lookout, you are the one who notices the nest, giant,
        some kind of raptor, and stops

wants to be beneath the girth of all those twigs and birthing — I appreciate this,
        his face when we were fucking or at the symphony painful with wonder,

that rapture I always seemed to watch, not participate in,
        not fully — every morning a different sand spit, today the tide could be further
                out than it's ever been
                            but I'm not sure.

The morning after it wasn't morning anymore

The morning after it wasn't morning anymore but evening
              always — him in the ice of your hand on my shoulder and the
river fugged with mist — I sat carelessly in my mind's night
              and repeated so this is it like a small

futile bird — this is it — there was no longing in me in that moment or
              perhaps the kind of longing a stone knows —
and the alders at the edge of the fog line still taller than going missing —

I, having little more to say, repeating so this is it, so —
              cannot even see as far as the inlet anymore, where it droops
into a slough ripe with skunk cabbage & rosehips — or maybe

it rises after all and there is a deeper room at the centre where
              what was said to each other has less relevance or even none
and pale ancient fish swim with some kind of what —

                                                            certainty.

Sundays, in the frozen construction site

Sundays, in the frozen construction site by the river, crows, on the gears, trailers,
    the still-raw mansard roofs, in the mud-ruts
and on the jimmied-together fence —

everything that honked & chugged now caws — is not static in pursuit, but flux,
    beautifully vague to us, a kind of apocalypse in reverse narration
        — all week long, I wonder

if I should leave you, because I say love and not in,
    that slight preposition signifying — the way the dog races for the water
to chase the ghost the gulls already consumed,

the mill chawed to dust — it can't help itself, you see — but I can — he was the
    tragedy that says everything changes fast so now
I don't want to hold onto a body at night and think yes,

forever happens while so near behind our window, the dark river rides the
    shoreline, draws some of the land into it, then further down
what was sunk into something like commitment

is dry on the banks again, incongruous amid the wildflowers, even more distant.

Suddenly, it's mid-December — the river

Suddenly, it's mid-December — the river clenches itself, fish bundle up in the
    mud — your grandfather is dead, his forgetting flown into the ether,
such relinquishment your sorrow or nostalgia or both
                  and you speak of leaves, burning —

I can't help you, in a sense, this is your grey moment — we don't all die in trucks
    by the side of the road, unnoticed for a day, as he did — but we all,
    invariably, fall solo out of this world, the brain eroding

            from its narratives, stories becoming

the kind of sand we have here — with bits of disconnected machine in it — a cog,
    a nail, something else unnamable to me — and so on — from the
shore's old mind I watch you alive, him dead, or just appear to be attached
         to resolution when, really, I could be that leaf too,

the bird's negative capability, intimate with what moves around me, towards, as
    I refuse to be distinct about what is air or water, both
evident forms of good, you see, and not those darknesses, dividing us,

                you choose to imagine.

The inexorable, the river, and the sounds

The inexorable, the river, and the sounds I hear and can no longer hear — machines,
    birdsong —
        if only they could spare that tree, or that one — or do they not want
            nests, any sweet capitulations —

        and if the answer wasn't so loud perhaps then I could listen to my
            blood, or you saying you've cried more with me than over the past
            eleven years — he is ghost, always, you know this —
        a moth landing damp on your arm in all the December rain is one —

        another, the eagle that passed so low over my head by the shore I could
            feel its talons and rising in its flight
        was hunger — the bear in the downtown dumpster, the deer that
            smashed through the window at the hardware store

        in the valley — tearing away the deep green feasts, the immune
                dens, we have torn — but I call to him as I shouldn't when
            you are entering me, or
maybe you don't mind — the three of us — dead, alive, alive and the river, dark
and past us,
                            ever-moving.

And now a swan by the shipyards, an otter

And now a swan by the shipyards, an otter, darkness slitting the surface, a white
 form skimming the rubber hulls — at dusk, everything

is blue, gold, buildings on fire at the horizon and the water
 a closer sky — the logs have so much rain in them but I sit

anyway and then crows in their vast black passages — we have little left to remind
 us we aren't alone — a ghost here, a ghost there — his, the others, a few

more — Mount Baker ripens just before night hits, the bridge lights come on —
 small painful fists —
 unclench unclench unclench —

I will always wish you could have endured.

They will disappear these ruins and this beauty too

They will disappear these ruins and this beauty too and this indistinguishable —
   I just wanted a raw place to wander in and for them also,

     a random spot — you can't find anything in townhouses & skyscrapers
     — O manicured & upright dwellings — there are no

        blackberries here, no sandpipers, no bullfrogs, no swallows' nests, no
            dead lobsters, no rotting fish, no old ropes

      or any other signs of history to speak of in copper or brick or steel
      or flesh — we are afraid for the children always — in this last

        undeveloped zone on Earth where the final species breathe — it
           is not enough to have everything — nothing

will soon be ours and the ads singing haven over the barren
        inhabited lands will show glorious faces,

glossy hands, bright feet — these will move down the sharp delineated
paths — these will not stop to feel — the empty river groomed for them

    as wallpaper,
        as screen — its mind only

                waiting for our absence.

Today the river is thick with wind

Today the river is thick with wind — a lifting, a clustering,
        a leaping up — the next day taut and holding everything —
solstice and a new cold blues the sky — missing him I have little

doubt this means I cannot love you too — today, I have little doubt —
        love is just too rampant for that, estuarial —
bringing him back I would wring all the poisons out of him and the memory even

of poison itself — then I would place him by the river and say breathe — breathe
        in, breathe out — for a very long time — and he would — it's hard
not to imagine cures & resurrections here — especially near this water

where I walk with you sometimes — how it takes the sounds of hammers,
        engines, sorrow and turns them into, not their inverse,
but to a kind of joy that acknowledges, draws these things into itself, says is,

okay,
                                    go on.

A tug passes and the river frays, splits

A tug passes and the river frays, splits —
                first thing in the morning: crescent moon, cormorant fishing
in darkness beneath the wharf —
                          crows begin their flight from the forest to
                          everywhere —

before work, you & I sat in bed, talked about — much — I like this time —
        wish it could have been the same with him — a sunrise calm — but
                wishing only twists me backwards —

                        grief I told you is always, but grieving — more
                            often intermittent —

the moon receding into blue — if they could only stop now — occluding beauty
    — but they don't — such bright ripe bands of cloud, that black mountain
    — alone again, or not really — ghosts, memories, the water

                        — everything holds me to it, says —
                                            speak.

Lots of trains today, their whistles

Lots of trains today, their whistles pooling — wet, wet the whole world greys,
    mucks itself, sloshes over and the river
    is the only Christmas I need — you reading a newspaper,

sipping a crème brûlée coffee in this slow-moments hour, he not here or here,
    who knows what the dead do, if they remain, somehow — I've felt
    him around, know he does — still the stones in my hand

stay silent, wefts of calcite, copper, the machines clenched in postures over
    openings into the earth — what will they do next, and us — will we
    retreat or deepen — during these times of flood, ducks

swash like flotsam in the current, bulrushes surge beneath the wharf — I feel
    happy right now — so much is water but little of it salt, its sudden
    claws sharp behind the eyes.

Given respite this morning,

Given respite this morning, a nerved quiet, black
fragments of crows passing, the thick pulse of headlights
behind the winter forest where the river curves towards
Surrey — only the foreman's truck pulls up, he yells, briefly,
into all that remains unfinished, drives away — you are gone,
for now, he is gone — much further — I miss his sweetness,
even though I know yours — two different kinds of tender and
the living can't compare to the dead anyway — you see how
they have stacked up rocks so you can't really reach the water,
stuck interpretive signs by the path, planted wild roses, a faux marsh
even — the loss of imperfect things cannot be measured — how his
snaggletooth grins in my mind or — fathomless, the river, for all its vast
intents, needs the cormorant on the pier to fix a dark
point of entry where the creatures of salt — you know them — begin.

Difficult today, the tears — and I see the river

Difficult today, the tears — and I see the river through them — sun swoons in the window,

slides a shape down the picture of his face on the dresser — long, honeyed rectangle of memory —

I look at it — awhile — doesn't stop — grief — just, grieving sinks inward, becomes moments more

subdued, quiet — now light pulls back into cloud, this big raw cumulus — and the river's less

postcard, more — itself — cold and dirty and mysterious — how much it endures of us as we build

and build our palaces, factories — listen — a train fastening the land — wishing I could jump on and ride

sometimes — as if I could escape thoughts of him that way — you are — not enough — but

then no one is thus it's only about — the insufficiency of blue in the sky right now — a slash here or is

that a sashay — nonetheless — first thing in the morning I have been misled already — the booms so

dark in the water they looked like pages in some history — what was, that is to say and not,

You make me ache river with your — let me say it

You make me ache river with your — let me say it — beauty — and the way

they've tortured you — you fill with
creosote & cadmium — minus signs swim
in your shallows — alongside your shores,
dump trucks line up like taxis, each allotted
two metal handfuls —

geese veeing through the plume from Lafarge — *this is why I came to Canada,*

you hear her say — all those booms
in the river — she thought it was
fascinating, the best part of geography — no,
nothing more romantic than the death of trees,
cells upon cells of them leashed — yarded

& those adorable little tugs called *Storm Surf,* called *Old School* — yes you make me

ache, river, because I cannot
save you and who am I to save
anyone — I couldn't even save
him, though he wrote — before
the last hit — that I was his

dark angel of mercy — yuck! — there is no subservient hope in these waters, beloved —

the birds scatter back from the woods,
trucks pull into the lot and it follows
its own fate — the river — burning again
with sunrise — as if it had never

                                                                        known grief.

Crow cries fall like snow after the snow

Crow cries fall like snow after the snowfall — the river doesn't hold the white —
                you in bed, palming a mug of coffee

— tears rake up — I can't help it sometimes — the wanting him
                to be here too — watching his happiness —

half-unfinished houses in the hush of Saturday and across the water,
                a pure bloom of ice on the fields

— why does this matter so much to me — recording it, getting it down,
                and yet never able to, really — when it's not loss,

the ineffable — well I want to say is joy — but not
                quite — that too can't be captured

— and now I'm just stumbling over my mind to reach you —
                to say the light is a kind of cold silk today,

that I can actually hear birds — to speak of nothing
                you haven't heard — in a sense —

but with a cadence including river, the uncertain, crying a bit
                here & there, a ghost for sure — a man

— and a witness at dawn — knowing it snowed
                all night, that the chronicle includes its melting.

Come to the window — you call to me

Come to the window — you call to me — I, wanting
              to sleep in, detach awhile from the beauty but, also,
              brood, and you know this so — come to the window,

you say — and it is as if the river is calling to me in its pale blue
              voice — snow again — thin but continuous — a hunkering
              down of mist over all those white, incomplete

dwellings, a myth made from weather — come to the window it says and
              witness — a sun-drizzle, this winter cumulus into
              the deepest part of the river, the wonk wonk

wonk of ducks, tetragon booms chained to the tails of tugs, snow in a scrim
              to the shoreline — not much — what speaks
              to me these days, gets me out of bed, beckons

come to the window — see — he's not alive anymore — see, he's everywhere —
              some principle of energy the river gathers together, holds.

The beach all geese today, slow sun dropping by

                        The beach all geese
today, slow sun dropping
by — I'm going to watch the river
into words! — I say before you leave and
you understand what I mean,

                        approve, even abet
the thing and I love this
about you — who wouldn't?
You know what grief
has done to my mind,

                        how the snow melts
at noon, freezes
overnight and dawn's pretty,
forbidding fields — I slipped
once on the ice with him —

                        he knew how fast
I can fall — irrelevant —
now he senses nothing —
maybe — tipped himself
out of the equation —

                        I wanted him to see this river —
have everything pure
again — if we weren't
taught the romantic version
of being human we might just

                        have a chance with ghosts — no,
stick to looking at
the water — it has such

umber light to offer you, those
crazy peaceful geese, sopping
marsh grasses, booms backed
with cold —

O, breathe.

Sweetheart, I say to the river — good morning, beautiful

Sweetheart, I say to the river — good morning, beautiful and I mean
him too, kissing his

soft ghost — though working in minus weather his winter lips were raw,
often bled, the men

in the luminous vests below suffer like he did — in other ways too — maudlin
I guess you're finding these —

revelations — three tugs dragging a lengthy boom of snow down past the
Blue House, the shipyards, beyond where

I can't watch anymore, dozens of white cylinders twisting in the current
and bovine mixers back up, pour their guts

onto the earth, make another parking lot, some hard place to land — language
is not enough, I get it, and I never said

nature cares if I stick its loveliness in a poem — just — what else does one
do with grieving — I can think of some poison

I could take — or a leap — but that's already been done — so I sit here at
dawn instead — craft a bit of music that is

nothing birdlike, nothing cadential as waves — only a small hum that has him
in it and you and serves as a greeting of sorts, a going on.

They call it a brownfield, but of course today

They call it a brownfield, but of course today, it's white — I raged
                at you last night — I raged and yet — I've
                forgotten how to destroy — to demolish and
                walk away relieved — this should be

a good thing — progress in the spirit and such — but how do they get
                those poisons out of the soil — let them sit —
                five, ten years — then they've leached so
                deeply down you can't scent them is all —

yes, this is a metaphor and no — the way the river today is not, or
                scarcely — furred by thin driblets of snow,
                a mist that mittens up the shipyard, the piers —
                could be a matte road this morning, current-less —

I depend too much on others, say this or nothing, pretend — furiously — what —
                that it matters — or doesn't — I shouldn't even be
                writing a poem at this moment — trying to — like
                the wildlife escape island they're building

in the middle of the Fraser because the Lord giveth after the Lord taketh away —
                those Old Testament developers — how nice all
                the animals will be, fixed in their marks
                on the stage, never straying and I just wanting a

wreck, really, if Elysium is done for
        — some beautiful ruin that humans will avert their eyes from

        but where birds alight
                          still.

Always, on opening your eyes, you gasp —

                                              Always, on opening your eyes, you gasp — beauty
at its clearest — a fierce winter sun ruching the argent waters — wind tipping
                                                        each ripple inside out so the
                                                                shimmer & grim

alternate while the boathouse remains in shadow — log booms arch hard limbs
                          into the current and the mountain unhinges itself
                                          from cloud, pierces cold, eternal as anything

                        we can imagine — beauty you said — is about surprise
though — and that, sometimes, is terrible as death — a veering away from the
    safe — witnessing to the difficult — the river part

solace and part a deepening of the dark animal — a poem that tells you it can be all
    as you are erased, chemical in its loveliness, harshly pelagic,

                                                      gorgeous with undertow.

A strange amber stain on the river this morning — what is it —

A strange amber stain on the river this morning — what is it — so much
that appears, disappears — we're not supposed to question — we consumers —
accept the effluent with the candy — don't ask why there are toxic waste containers
on the shoreline — corporations don't play neighbour — you won't get pie
or an aspidistra out of them — meanwhile workers sing Paganini in the guts
of unfinished townhomes — he was one of them, hard hat inked with days,
slapped with stickers — Talk Shit, Spit Blood — it's a hard world, don't you
forget it, kid — though the sun has dribbled out of the clouds now — boing,
boing, boing — and you're Mr. Sweet-As-All-Get-Out — and the cat didn't quite
break my toe when I tripped over it last night — simple mercies at coffee time where
I sit staring at the water, wondering about this & that — crows surfing the light
out to Richmond —

Does the river need me, I wonder

Does the river need me, I wonder
after reading Steve Heighton's line —

*the world may not need poets, but the earth
does* — if not then, why, at this time,

have I been placed here, so positioned
with my words, my camera, to record,

bring some account of the senses to —
whomever — if so — but this can't be —

no matter how imperilled nature is, this
gorgeous, tormented river — it still

doesn't need me — cannot — I lose
respect at servility — even implied —

though nature may win — a bit — if
a poem does what he writes — *substantiate it,*

redeem it, render it tangible again — I paraphrase
here — nature is not on the side

of the poem — or of the killers — the river,
with its dual currents, pulses past the construction

site, through the estuary to the salt as it
always has, while the metal claw fastens

once more to its shoreline and my pen
makes little dark aches on the page.

Happy Valentine's Day river and you too of course

Happy Valentine's Day river, and you too of course who brought me eggs in bed
this morning — dry but well-meant — and him — in absentia — who
two years ago wrote in a card — *To a new life* — before dying — his words etched
ironic on my flesh — *love always, again* — what does this mean — to have
such feelings cancelled and yet continue on in other forms — you so
different — in age, physique, desires — to him — though kin with
sweetness I suppose — which is what matters — and the capacity to
endure, adore, despite — as I used to write to him — despite everything,
thanks for — would the river write this letter — I think not — it
doesn't need to forgive or be forgiven, to proclaim allegiance
with a ring, blooms, bonbons or the like — yes it is our fault it has oil in it
and nails, yes it is beautiful at dawn — there is so much they cannot see of
what was both beauty & dark — who has love enough in them not to judge

       — the strange salt in its floods

                                          its mysterious tidal reaches.

The river is so beautiful today I have no choice

                        The river is so beautiful today I have no choice
but to write again — that equinoctial light dropped
       through the cumulus in one

                    concentrated forge on the waters where all the silver
in the world is melted and dark boats pass through
       and are changed — I can tell you don't

                  believe me, but it happens — when grief appears
you know this as more a chemical descent than
       anything, wait for it to rise — you don't

                  die like he did, suffering an extreme of loneliness —
no — nor do you flee from love not being like it was, those old & fabled
       definitions — I've seen you watching the river for hours,

                  poet, and though the light constantly
changes, never once is it ugly or
       without that total understanding
                                    of home.

A short line of ducks flying fast

A short line of ducks flying fast
across the river like frenzied black protractors almost — every morning — makes

me weep — how hard everything
must work to survive us — they cannot land here — machines — or there —

coils of wire, rebar and even in the waters
their feet & feathers are likely to glow with a sheen of motor oil — nowhere

immune — this is the premise — and
nowhere divested of him either — though often it's only what killed him that attends

me in my nightmares — tearing at my
flesh with its reminder — I got to him last — he's my final groom not yours —

there's only a fine membrane of a door
between worlds and nothing between us and nature — but we have designed

ourselves to create barriers, it is our
forte now — no ghosts and no ducks — flickering past our vision, flying over —

Achingly beautiful — I understand this now —

Achingly beautiful — I understand this now — the river in May with its blue & grey shirring and all the swallows that have returned slipping over it — the fluid air, tiny dark nests in the stucco — even the machines move softly now, shrunken by the lush green leaves — and I never stop wishing he could see this — *pretty* — he would have exclaimed — his gangly smile widening with such brief extremes of happiness — exquisite vistas always provoking the thought — this, no this, could have saved him — ineradicable ghosts in me — even through your forgiveness, guilt — how can I start again — the river does though — it busts out of winter once more — refusing the scraped raw trees, ice fixing its trajectory — any further negotiations with the cold.

The rain, machines but I remember —

                    The rain, machines but I remember — on the shoreline
                        last night —

a sandpiper —

                    how just at sunset — that smudge-down of red & swarthy
                        pinks — it had

stopped

                    its frantic ticking among stones and was plumped upon a
                        splinter from one of those

dark

                    logs — so still — even as I moved closer — only its slow head
                        stirring, that

beak

                    a notch of black — aloof to the barking herons, the swallows
                        who are river made

flesh

                    as they skirr the evening for midges, their convulsive lack of
                        beauty — even the long

breath

                    of a crescent moon — all this and a tug, the Ken McKenzie
                        — yawping out

diesel

                    log drivers leaping shadows upon the booms, chain clanks and
                        a guttural chug

away —

                    the sandpiper not like anything human — him and you and I
                        vanishing — and it,

waiting

                    for the day — maybe or, not vigil, not witness — no sandpiper,
                        we have no

language

                    to say this, you see.

And what if, after all this, river

And what if after all this, river, I have not appreciated you enough —
which will always happen — that feeling of insufficient ability to
stop your death — looking at him in old

pictures in the light rising from the filtered-through morning and saying
over & over again — he was so beautiful — as if this is part of the
pact of living on — that saving softness to the lips,

his chest's eternal tightness — surely this will prove resurrectable,
return to me — and I can reverse the poisoning of the soil, how
rampant garbage is on the sleek crests of still-innocent sand

— no, stupid — what's done is done — and in his story — outside
recuperation — the river though — there is something we want to imagine
lies always beyond us forgiving transgression — crooning I know

I know I know you cannot be other than you are and on the furthest
side of your pain I will keep the herons, preserve the tansy,
hold the bright fish — leaping —

The Last Aubade

Everything is silver this morning — not only the river — everything —
the mud, the new unfurnished homes, our cats, my feelings for you —
I'm not afraid to say this — I know little — and I can imagine too many possible
lives to perhaps properly inhabit any of them

— but also — love is a wealth in me —

and beauty breaks against all pain without cease — everything is silver — and so
this is more a rant or a chant than a poem — I don't care anymore what
things are called or how they get fixed in the mind — only that they
rupture me — not like death but like living on afterwards and knowing why —

this I know at least — that I can still see when everything is silver
— and call out to you and you echo me — or even bring me to the edge of sight
first — there is nothing perfect between us —
we have each lived too many pasts

— but I would rather this now than a story I never
really planned to tell anyway — you understand — and everything —
even the crows this morning — are silver — their wings — as
they twist backwards into the gleam — catching

the days we have left together — silver you could say as scars, or age,
or ashes — silver as what holds everything this morning

— after all we've been through — over the always-silver river.

Conniption: The River

1.

Split and raucous with light it wings past us. The river yields pale & dark, pale & dark variants, then a tug. You sleep on and I cover you, juxtapose you with what is lost. The point being, not an already thing and thus. It's as if we are seeing the insides of trees everywhere. Dust in a backwards veil hovers, then is sprayed down. Depression is like a sheath, he says, the eyeball opens, you live in it, water flicks up on the banks; you feel nothing. Even the fruit could be cast away. Then, the fetal happens. So you can wait beyond concepts of waiting. I'm telling him — the grief regions are vast. I may call out *hello hello I live only here now* but the truth is a geography. Saw whinges. Click of trucks. The overexposed heron doesn't calibrate quickly. Lollop of otter. Fish whipping and the elusive option that this is not, again, a hook. Falling 1000 feet into your memory. The claw marks on the faux leather loveseats resemble insane constellations. Vagabond heart, always. Though I drizzle the tomato plant every day. The hummingbird, virulent, hurts.

2.

The mud hisses, hushes on the low-lying beach. Seriously more a sluice though for ghosts, wastes passing from the chi-chi bowels of new urban dwellers, the faint stink always where machines were, the mill, dead forests do-si-do-ing from pylon to pier, souls set to rapid Lucreatian decay, abreacting.
I'm happy today, you tell me. We picked blackberries bowering over cement wreckage. We engaged in a simple conversation about baking with an elderly pair of sportifs, so navy & white in the sunshine. There is the chance we will survive to participate in such a duet: the sawhorse on the roof yearning, weeds playing competitively on the deserted volleyball courts. O gasp, a blue moon, then an orange one. The apocalypse promises aestheticism after all though he's not around to see it. I shy away from his likeness, looking to the furry clouds instead, to birds I identify by the curves of their wings, the speed at which they mitigate all suffering.

3.

Guessing the look on a corpse's face is not transcendence but devoid, I still, staring at the river with crows rowing over it or through the burr of first sun, smell him some days. Smokes & gum mostly. Sense him around — a spectral swelling in the room — just another contradiction at the supermarket. Like building wilderness island: a place where birds stay! The grid descends, clicks into place and all my efforts to write nonsense have failed. Sound is a holy toil but not the only cat & stuffed-parakeet-on-a-rope trick. Perhaps a withering glance is what you give me at this point, I ensconced in my aerie of language while you deal with the plebes again, texting and perishing everywhere, until you wish you'd been born with your retinas gouged out. Every log boom has a silver lining however and on this morning in the initial ruckus of September, I want to honour those who have more dead in their kaffeeklatsches than living. Growing old, as Oppen noted, is a strange thing to happen to the young, blackberries pinking somehow wrinkled fingers, the tongue holding the cold fruit as long as it can.

One Haiku; Four Takes
    after Diane di Prima

Early morning fog
Six crows circle the river
Seeking the lost trees

The thinned-out forest
Even sparser amid fog
Six crows; six shadows

A burr of pale fog
Six dark hearts, falling towards
The treeline; no trees

Somewhere, a river
Somehow, the fog-tamped woods
Here, six crows, turning.

One January Morning

Long dark necks of geese hyphenate the fog
and then the light bears down on the river.

I remember what it was like to be born.
It took a long time and the same fish-tinsel of sun

broke my eyes open to the world beyond the artificial mirrors
through which my head was seen, crowned with its regal vulva.

In the hills of Cappadocia, plastic water bottles roll
slowly in the sand, their violent migration accumulating.

I can't tell you what it's like to accept things.
Some days, a black vellum is just peeled back from your heart

and, silly as it sounds, you are both raw and unafraid of being hurt,
coffee tastes amazing, the Chinese lantern tree glows on the balcony,

and you begin this difficult, unfinishable poem.

Catch & Release

Imagine them
               down there — the sturgeon —
lonely trawlers in the benthic gloam, moving through the dark below us for over
    100 million years,
         sleek
                 cartilaginous dreams, fish witnesses and now
we serve them up
             until they are scarce, pop out their roe, discard the heavy old
                bodies, pose
with trophied remainders, say
        the head was massive as a wine barrel
say
        it felt like holding a dinosaur
say
        this guy has been alive since Confederation, all eighteen
           ugly feet of him
six of them stationed along the white flesh, gumboots in the muck, gloves
    pressed
        against its scutes, barbels trailing the unreadable surface
             of the river.   But what do we know
of its polypoid mysteries, how its rostra was shaped by its anadromous passage,
    this ancient
            bony *Huso*
        caught twice in one season, can you believe our luck?
Now the hook weaseled out from the lip,
            the desecrated weight of it all
returning.

Reversals

I watch the river through the leaving winter of the trees —
soon the webbed droop will green and water un-filigree itself
become more solid chunks of silver between the plushed-out alders
planted skimpily along the carefully rip-rapped shoreline —

Grief is careful in me now too I think — doesn't gush its garish past but
knows stone, this necessity, a bank of rock where weeds leak, drops
ooze but infrequently, at intervals, while to the eye — palisades, moat —
not less a tribute — three years since — seasons shift through chill, monsoon,

emerge bloomingly without negation — I see him, a kind of Spring in my mind
every day while having held him ash — the one does not erase the other —
a river leafs out beautifully —
                            the trees become heavy with flood.

One History of the Fraser

Up the river to the smelter — the topography of what we wanted — bronchial
carcass of car husks, once lavishly buffed, now a ludic mass,

strata upon strata of glommed-together metal: white, blue & red predominant,
shelled parts hooked with insect unhappiness, beetle-glinted

in a sun that forgives them their ugliness, our disposable sorrows.

*

We don't ask what happens after our desire pinnacles and then the cold
sets in. Past us floats *The Sea Warrior*, its hull linked

to an empty barge; the current whips them fast through our daydream
and we are relieved only that a small moment of nothing

has gone by.

*

Anticipating the temperature to stretch to its full catastrophe on the height chart,
there is a wanted apocalypse in us.

We would get our relentless Greek tragedy then yes, wars for water, our hearts
spoiling without Freon's luxury, or biblical locusts for air.

We love the idea of comeuppance, guilt's expatiation in disaster, the river
wrecking even our fantastic high-rises as it swells

over us, and no escape finally from the dark.

*

Now only a buoy's orange period ends & ends & ends each wave.
As if they had never been trees, the log booms externalize themselves

in squares. Here the river is grey though when we name it silver it will
rear itself backwards through childhood and we can ride the wet memory

that was us, residing along the shorelines, a humble peaceable race, content
as the textbooks write, with the crayfish, the saltless walleye, squatting

in our circular huts, fires beaded & re-beaded against the night.

"Love should not be written in stone, but in water"
$$\text{Catullus}$$

In the wake of the passing, another wake.
The water does not return to itself.
There is a gleam, a density.
The sun pivots in the wound

where a white bird retires its flying.
Perhaps I will drown before the succulent
impossibility is uncovered, that the fluid
mind writes & rewrites its borders

and the red barge only seems like stone.
Forgive me, distant progeny, I might cry,
for needing to live as a tributary
cued by the kinds of weather

the primitive blood fears.
But you won't recall who I was anyway —
your rogue wave ancestor who made
beauty within the ruins

& spent her days taking a river
into her eyes, drenching the pages

with salt & creosote & devotion.

What they call this

Man fragile with chemicals

I miss you on this effervescent day, hot October slowing over the river
    where the small, slate boats yank salmon nets whose
dark beads draw birds and one female eagle in the opposite

cottonwoods cries a sound I interpret as loneliness —

That's what I have become — translator of the world's grief, sifter of your dopamine
    sorrow — four years and still, I wept in the shower
this morning, raging out your absence, recalling your silly,

wet-slick happiness as we soaped

each other to an instant's glossy reversal —
Everything you were now ash, memory, my mind can't depart — they call this
    difficult mourning — those specialists in loss —

if I could have juggled your serotonin descents,

recalibrated those tiny, violent receptors —
    there is always this pointless set
of questions — the water extending its silver moment, withdrawing it.

Phantomnul

The liquid tin light of early morning is already a soft corrosion by nine
and the ghosts are breaking open on the river.
You capstan. You gunwhale.
You that green wound clicked off at dawn.
I used to see their bodies as cartoon or part of the ungreat chain of despoilers
yet now they are solid little specters of a dwindling narrative
tire-haloed bows & a hull of salt, yanking the tired barges across
inlets, estuaries, arterial passages,
empty or pale with cremains, dieseling their engines of the afterlife
beneath the black nineteenth century dream.
You funnel. You bollard pull.
You pushboat of the ephemeral end.

The River System
after Louise Cotnoir's *Archipelago (17 islands)*

On the River of Disabusement
trickles are sluggish
there is no need to tell me again
that my boat
will not crest
on childhood's shoreline
or make it
to the glittering falls
where tickets are sold
and replicas.

It's okay.
I can take this infidel newspaper instead.
Let's not tarry.
Let's push on.

*

Sorry but
Mud River
is closed for
this season and
likely others.
You cannot see
your face in it,
the compass stutters;
in your fists great handfuls
of the system clump,

refuse to hold your vessels,
envisaging some lost,

inauspicious
beauty.

*

Mornings,
where what
is held there
is eternal
velour, resists
transmigrating
into flocks or memories
or is, otherwise, silver.
This is your
River of Solace
and I fear it because
what of it lasts, but demurs
after the lunch hour, evanescing.

*

So haunt me,
River that Will Not Consign Itself to the Shallows.
There are vacant fish
who swim in you, their slow pelagic eyes
stirring, a category of aquatic
emptiness I have familiarized
myself with and now

how to sum up the spectres,
those bottom feeders that arrive
upon the announcement
of ashes.

*

Loosely attuned to the weather
around this little boat,
I sense a deluge of recklessness
on the horizon.
Pardon me, dead man, for I
have given in to thunderstorms when,
sinking a bit further,
I might have encountered shoals of Edenic
serenity or transparencies of sunshine.

I couldn't risk it you see,
and that's the way it
always is in the rapids
of Slipping River.

*

Chagrin River sounds
almost content though
it's offering its regrets often —
no it cannot attend the absolute
miasma of the present and the future's
mired soiree is unlikely too
but the past? Now that place it weaves
between — those sour shores are
somehow lovely to it —

they are already part of a story
that has flooded the body
but — not quite —
moved on.

*

Today I began to think —
if I were only staring out

upon land, I would be
heartbroken — yes the mind
is avid for such pronouncements,
plans for a desert and the
impossibility of enduring but in fact
the River of the Ineffable Bloodline
cannot really be looked at,
it is a wet thread in the duvet,
a damp channel of reverie. See

out your window, it is prehistorically
dry or from a future where it rushes
through a last forest
long beyond you.

*

The River of the Dissolving Moon
watches our latest fight.
We state perhaps it's all over
and are absolute as humans can be.
The water flows past in its light
then the light renews itself
for the duration.
You must imagine, the river suggests,
that it is not planet nor absence
but the one converging

within the other's ability
to yield. Do we dismiss
this lesson though the rays
are honey in our blood?

*

It is rush hour again
in my feelings for him.
Down Teeming River, small
boats of once-was pass
freighters of what-if, horns
echoing through black shallows,
gases writing monotonous
sentences in the air.
Standing beside this waterway,

you will never notice
how the clouds above you are few
& minor, that time shifts
in its unpredictable dalliances.

*

O River is not circular; it does
not meet its own beginnings. O
River has no pretensions to wholeness,
knowing such quests lead
back to the ragged shoreline.
You will never entirely appreciate
O River, which is what gave it
this name.
When the explorer stood
on the prow of his hunger,
gazed upon the solitary waters
flooding his mind and uttered
O River, O

River, the appellation held
like any ghost's embrace, both
the letter of it
and the feeling.

*

When light overwhelms
my sorrow, please
forgive me.
Grief is a tedious land,
until sleep, with its serpentine
detachments, prevents me from taking
yet another number in my wait
for happiness.
Instead, the dark banks
enclose me with their reeds
& marsh grasses and in the water

of all that is nearly saltless,
I am peaceful.
This is what they call
The River of Night-Time Consolations.

*

Lest you believe
I own no other symphony
than mourning,
the River of the Funny Chuckle
comes to rescue us.
It is only a short waterway
to be sure
but so characteristic, so clear
that once you have heard its burble
there will never be again,

in any moment of sorrow,
the off-chance that it will not
visit you with its pure
& ridiculous joy.

*

Longing River
but for what
the body wants
to know
yet the water withholds.
Suffice to say

it flows towards
a destination that
cannot be seen, that it
does not even desire.

*

What's becoming sadly familiar
is the River of Invisible Fish.
It races through our shopping malls
and doesn't drop anything off.
In the streets, shoals of cars
swim through it and otherwise
it's famous for its emptiness,
the way it allows you to pretend
the water will bloom with food
and then provide no illusion

of repast, offer you
nothing but your face
reflected & reflected
again.

*

The River of Before & Never Since
wants to be renamed.

At night it courses through
your body, rippling with alternate
baptisms. Possibly it could
become the River of Before & Always,
or the River of Once & Its Repetitions

or even the bright River of Excess
and in this manner, the same red boat
will be attending you, unmoored,
down the rapids.

*

Untranslatable River
utters the dark countries
it passes in your blood
and though you recognize
the ports, the docks, those
homes bordering the flood-line,
when you wake you cannot
imagine why you stopped

to visit such lands, the light
wipes out the river and your tongue
feels heavy as earth
in your mouth.

*

What if I told you
there is no river, that
on looking out my window
I see only an expressway, a meadow,
the face of a ghost.
What if I said,
there has never been any river

but only wartime, a half-price
sale, bullying in the schoolyard.
What if I wrote,
rivers such as these don't exist
and there is only a small stain
on the rug, the coffee pot's burn,
a hunger in me for the poem
beyond words.

Well at that point you'd have
to reply — what you're talking about
is the River that Still Flows Where
There is no River — and you'd be right.

Acknowledgements

Earlier versions of some of these poems have appeared in *Canary*, the *Montucky Review*, *Earthlines*, *Planet Earth Poetry*, *Barzakh*, the *Alfred Gustav Press*, *Eunoia*, the *Malahat Review*, *Thrush Poetry Journal* and *CNQ*.

With deep thanks to Michael Holmes and the conscientious crew at ECW for honouring my poems of grief and to the Owen family, for always being there.

© Michael Belandiuk

CATHERINE OWEN was raised in Vancouver and lives in Edmonton. She has published 15 collections of poetry and prose. *Dear Ghost* was nominated for the Pat Lowther Award and won the Alcuin Prize. *Locations of Grief*, her memoir anthology featuring 24 Canadian writers, is also forthcoming in 2020.

Get the eBook free!*
*proof of purchase required

At ECW Press, we want you to enjoy this book in whatever format you like, whenever you like. Leave your print book at home and take the eBook to go! Purchase the print edition and receive the eBook free. Just send an email to ebook@ecwpress.com and include:

- the book title
- the name of the store where you purchased it
- your receipt number
- your preference of file type: PDF or ePub

A real person will respond to your email with your eBook attached. And thanks for supporting an independently owned Canadian publisher with your purchase!